Slices of

Mary-Frances Hewlett

Slices of life

Mary-Frances Hewlett

Mary-Frances Hewlett

This edition copyright © 2025

Cover design & artwork

Juliana Kotuličová

Slices of life

Slices of life

Introduction

This is a just a little collection of anecdotes from normal life. Well, not normal really because that would be boring I think. Okay, so every day stuff. Yeah, that sounds better. Apart from The Three Wise Woman which is obviously fiction. (But inspired by a Christmas card I saw)

Flippin' heck this introduction lark is more difficult to write than the actual book.

Let's try again.

Sixty-one year old idiot woman finally writes her first book and she hopes it makes you smile.

Bingo.

Dedication

This little book is dedicated to My Magnificant Seven: William, Edward and James - still my three heartbeats and so proud of you all.

Aurora, Catherine and Jan - my Warrior Queens. Thank you.

The Legendary June Woodward - who cared enough to write my children's heights on her kitchen wall as they were growing up. It meant the world.

Mary-Frances Hewlett

14th February 2025

JANUARY

Cheese & Pickles and Paul Newman's Bum

New Year's eve was lovely and joyous and we pigged out on homemade quiches and shop bought potato wedges and mountains of coconut ice.

By 2am we both had indigestion and heartburn and were farting enough to slay a dragon.

When you're a sloth by nature, you need to be with someone who understands, nay Embraces, the blissful state of doing sod all on a day off. New year's Day we were Olympic Champions at it.

Slouched on the sofa, occasionally holding hands when

said hands weren't reaching for the Quality Street, sausage rolls and a lovely variety of cheeses and pickles, we scanned the TV schedules for a mutually agreed film to watch.

This is easier said than done as all couples will know. He said no to Bridget Jones, Pride & Prejudice or anything where people unexpectedly break into a song and dance number wearing either legwarmers or crinolines.

I said no to cars being transformed from dumpster to dream machine, presented by white rappers with bad jokes and questionable taste in gold chains. You know who you are.

Aha.....The Towering Inferno. Quality disaster. 1970's fashions. The legendary Fred Astaire. Trying to remember who gets out alive. Plus, and more importantly, the very winning combination of Steve McQueen dressed as a fireman and Paul Newman being .....well, Mr Paul Newman.

Settling down to watch the developing disaster, I had warm (excuse the pun) memories of my father quizzing me when it used to be shown on the telly in my teenage years. Dad used to constantly check my fire prevention knowledge as due to our remote location , fire safety was paramount. We'd all be burnt to a crisp before Fireman Sam had even slid down his pole otherwise.

Dad would interrupt my viewing (even at 14, I ssem to recall I had a very healthy appreciation of Mr Newman) and ask random questions like: Why shouldn't he have opened that door? What did he add to the Fire Triangle?

By the way, the explosion happened because when he opened the door, the air was added to the Fire Triangle and caused the fire to expand. Fire needs air, something to actually burn and heat. Thank you very much. Girl Guide Firefighters badge 1975. Top marks. Coached by Dad.Oh and the idiot security guard in the film who opened the door was played by OJ Simpson. Not sure if he wore gloves on that occasion either.

Slices of life

So...Steve McQueen is looking all smokey and understated and a tiny bit grubby. Sigh. Nice helmet.

Paul Newman is rescuing children that he doesn't know and kissing Faye Dunaway who he loves (but not enough to give her his jacket, I've noticed. Poor Faye looking a tad chilly in her 70's evening gown from Brentford Nylons)

Richard Chamberlain is the selfish baddie and he's wearing a frilly shirt. He is William Holden's dastardly son in law and has cut corners building the tower bit of said Inferno title and it's all his fault. But then he does something Really Despicable. Are you ready for this?

He jumps the bloody queue. I kid you not.

That would never happen in England. My Gran queued for three hours in 1944 because the corner shop had a delivery of bananas. If Richard Chamberlain had behaved so badly then he'd have throttled by twenty furious housewives all carrying gas masks.

I loved him in Thorn Birds and The Slipper & The Rose but when he kicked everyone out of the way and clamboured onto the rescue chair I booed him. When he plummetted to his death, we cheered.

Paul Newman bent over a lot, rescuing people or checking fuses. Even in beige polyester slacks, he has A Very Nice Bum.

Eventually (spoiler alert) Steve McQueen and Nice Bum, er I mean Paul Newman blew up the water tanks.

My fellow sloth and I discussed the flaws in this solution at length as there seemed many. You'd surely need an ocean to put this fire out? and can dear ol' Fred Astaire swim?

I must admit my arguments died a little when both heroes tied themselves to pillars with rope in readiness of the water tanks exploding. I even stopped eating for a few minutes.The floods came and the fire was miraclously put out. Steve and Paul, plus Faye in her frock and darling

Slices of life

Fred all survived. Plus the cat. (The cat always survives. Ever watched Aliens?)

We both expressed our disbelief, even though we'd seen the film dozens of times before. Several mugs of builders tea, more cheese and pickles and a wedge of chocolate cake while we pulled apart the American Film Industry.

Came to the satisfying conclusion that in the Uk, we'd have sent in James Bond & Harry Potter with Neville Longbottom (because we love him) and before long it'd have been sorted and kettle on for a brew and the dying embers used to toast teacakes.

But there's a downside. No polyester slacks.

FEBRUARY

Author's note: I've been on several disasterous dates in my lifetime and some very lovely ones. As Valentine's Day is in February, this very memorable date seems appropriate to share with you.

The only dates I'd be willing to go on these days are a lock in at Cadburyworld or an Arsenal season ticket game.

Stuart

I had a lunch date yesterday. Anything that involves food with me is generally a good idea (no kidding, Mary, really?!) and when Stuart, 55 suggested meeting up via the dating app, I thought why not? Be brave !

Anyhow, I slapped on some face, shaved the moustache and even brushed my hair. I put myself out to be pleasant and smiley. Added extra was the gorgeous bus driver from days of old taking me into Exeter. I suspect though that my lazy eye went a-wandering, as he kept looking behind him when I smiled at him.

Well, Stuart was attentive. Bless his heart. He was very polite and charming and smelt clean. Did I mention that Stuart was attentive?

He turned up with flowers and chocolates. Lovely to be given both, obviously. But this was in the middle of Exeter High Street. People must have thought we were making a movie.

He hugged me like I was a lifebelt on the Titanic.

Called me Little Lady. Now by no stretch of anyone's imagination am I little. NASA can probably see me from space. I can be ladylike however, but only in short intervals. Shocker, I'm still single, eh?!

After five minutes he called me His Little Lady. I had to gently remind him that we were just meeting for lunch, not having our banns read. By this time, I'm eyeing up the exits in the restaurant. He wasn't nasty or creepy. Just very very earnest to treat me like a china doll. Oh stop laughing you lot.

Lunch was a nightmare.

S: What would you like, my little lady?

China Doll: Quiche and salad would be lovely, thank you

S: Are you sure?

CD: Yes absolutely, thank you

S: (to Hovering Waitress) Excuse me, what pastry is the quiche?

HW: Short.

S: Oh right, not puff? Hmmmm is that okay for you, Mary?

(By now, I'm wanting to crawl under the table. Hovering waitress is glaring at him and then looking at me as to say: Where the fuck did you find *him*?!!)

I tuned out for a moment.

S: Now, what about a filling?

(CD inwardly freaking out. Filling? Does he mean sex? Shiiiiittttttt. Oh! he's still talking about the bloody quiche. Thank God.)

HW: It's broccoli, cheese and ham.

CD: That sounds delicious, thank you so much

S: What cheese would that be? Do you like all cheeses, my little lady?

CD: Yes, I love all cheese except Stilton, but I quite like it in a quiche.

S: (looking at the HW worriedly) Ahh....is it...?

HW: (growls) No, it's bloody cheddar, extra mature !

S: That'll be lovely for you, Little Lady.

Hovering waitress looks at me, her eyebrows raised into her hairline. I can see what she's thinking. You? Little? Seriously? I wasn't offended. It's like giving Victoria Beckham the nickname Smiley. Nope.

While we wait for our meal, I try to make conversation but it's tricky. He's looking at me the same way I gaze at Choux Buns. Absolute longing.

When the food arrived, Stuart cut all of his food into small pieces first. He then proceeded to only use the fork to eat while reaching over the table to hold my hand with his spare one.

I wriggled my hand free, apologising for needing to use both my knife and fork. He still gazed at me adoringly. It was very offputting. And for me, very very unusual.

I asked him about his life and interests as his profile had been a little vague apart from books and walks. He didn't really want to talk about himself much, bless his heart. He said he was lonely and his mother was 88 and he was devoted. I kept thinking of the shower scene in Psycho.

He asked me about my interests so I embellished a bit to make me sound quite threatening – tai kwondo, kick boxing and shot put. I also made my three sons sound like Peaky Blinders meets The Krays. I wanted Stuart to come to his own conclusion that we weren't suited. I can be the biggest cow in the world but I don't like hurting nice people's feelings.

At the end of our lunch (no pudding, I could not face that poor HW again) I thanked him politely for a lovely time and it had been nice to meet him. I chose my words very carefully.

He held my hand tighter than Alan Rickman at the end of Die Hard.

We must meet up again, he said with anguish. I want a relationship with you !

(I want Hugh Jackman but that's not going to happen either, flower)

He was very keen. We went for a little stroll around the cathedral green, me somewhat hindered by the huge bouquet I'm carrying. People thinking she's either about to get married or throw herself onto a coffin as an hysterical mourner.

I gently suggested to Stuart that we didn't have that spark and that I work ridiculous shifts so meeting up would be difficult.

He nodded in agreement.

Yes, Mother said you would be working a lot but she liked that you work in a nursing home so you know all about lifting and bowels and suchlike. On your days off you could always stay over, little lady. Separate rooms, of course. Mother is worried about breaking a hip, you see. She liked your profile, you see.

Ah yes Stuart, I do see.

Mind you Mary, he added worriedly. You hadn't mentioned before that you did the shot put.

MARCH

Iceland Adventures

So........quick trip to Iceland this morning (the shop not the country)

Does anyone remember when it used to Bejam? (the shop not the country) Mind you, it's quite the holiday destination these days (the country, not the shop)

Sorry I digress.

Timed the visit to coincide with the bus timetable so had list (fairly usual) and enough money on card (fairly unusual) so zoomed around in military fashion, focused and not even glancing at the frozen gateaux and packs of

Slices of life

16 eclairs. I know !

Only one checkout open of course and the little old ladyin front of me had a small loaf and a banana milk and the guy in front of her had A Trolley Full. Packed to the rafters.

He very kindly invites the pensioner to go in front of him and she thanks him nicely. I try to look old and dithery (not tricky...my roots needs doing and I've got my shopping trolley with me for the bus ride home later) but nope, he's having none of it. He proceeds to unload the Mount Etna of provisions.

£246 !! In Iceland !! You've gotta be going some to spend that outside of Christmas.

To be fair to him, he unpacked his trolley and repacked into bags with precisin and skill and coordination.

I thought blimey, I bet his missus is a satisfied woman.

So I'm back out by the bus stop with a good 10 minutes to spare for my return journey.

Nope. Make that 60 minutes spare as said bus had broken down.

My fellow waitee was a guy from Lancashire. Man, he was loud (and I'm deaf) He decided to have a phone conversation with his entire contacts list, going through each one and talking very very very loudly.

I dare not move away in case the phantom bus should make an appearance so prayed that he would get sick of waiting and start walking. Nope.Every call ended with him saying Yeah bye bye bye bye bye bye bye bye........bye.

Bus finally arrived just as I was searching for a blunt instrument.

An Hour, People. An Hour. He.Did.Not.Draw.Breath.

I sent thanks Up for my salvation.

Well I'm guessing God didn't get my message because he

carried on chatting on the bus to.........me.

Chatty Man: That were a long wait for t'bus

Mary Soon To Be Serial Killer: It certainly was.

CM: You going t'wimborne then?

MSTBSK: Yes.

CM: How long have you lived there then?

MSTBSK: Not long

(icy glares that can freeze anyone at 100 yards having absolutely no effect on him at all)

CM: Why did you move?

MSTBSK: Pardon?! (I'd heard him, just was gobsmacked by his nosiness)

Because I decided to.

CM: Do you know what stop you need? Well you being new here you probably don't. I know Wimborne really well. I come from Bury but we moved here when I were 16. Haven't lost the accent have I ? This covid thing is just a big con I reckon, just to make us all buy more bog roll. It's school holidays this week so I told my missus I'd get t'shopping and you look after kids. She phoned me......

MSTBSK: Blimey, she was lucky to get through

CM:...........and said pick up some cat litter coz the kitten has shat on the bedroom carpet again. I told her it's a cat that's what they do. Oh you getting off?

Yes I answered, very very gratefully. It's my stop.

Home for a much needed cuppa and wishing I'd bought those bloody eclairs.

APRIL

Happiness & All Things Haggis

So here's the thing. Me and Mr O have been together a fair few months now and it's going nicely. He likes my cooking and that I enjoy watching Match of the Day. I like his hugs and humour. So we're both thinking let's see where this goes.

Well this going to Scotland on our first holiday together. I'm ticking the days off on the calendar and he says he is too. He's been before but loves all things Scottish. I've a hankering to try haggis.

I announced to my offspring and one of my besties

Catherine of the impending week in the Highlands and there was a collective silence. Conversations were shared by simply eye rolling.

Eldows were nudged. Which one to speak first?

Eldest son Will, voiced his opinion:

Holy shit Mother. He'll kick you out of the car before Salisbury !!

General agreement, nodding of heads. To make matters worse, they were eating MY food too.

I was dumbfounded. Kick me out of the car? Why? I'm a delightful travelling companion. Get some music on and I'm suddenly Adele at the O2. He'll get a full blown concert as we head up t'north.

(I've never been further north than Liverpool ...I get giddy anywhere past Taunton. Can I use English money? Sorry, I digress)

They then made enquiries about the type of accomodation

we'd booked. A two bedroomed cottage next to a loch, I stated proudly.

Everyone nodded with more enthusiasm amd I beamed at them, feeling slightly redeemed from the departure at Salisbury comments.

Ed observed: At least he'll have somewhere to hid the body. Those lochs are deep.

Everyone murmurs in bloody agreement !!

Catherine would be my ally I was sure. She'd been on holidays with me to Corfe Castle for the past five years. She'd back me up.I asked her if I was stressful to spend a week with in a cottage?

She studied her shoes very intently, avoiding my eyes

No.....she said vaguely. But I can get to Birmingham if you need collecting.

Oh cheers for that, Cath.

More questions: Will there be wifi coverage at this place, Mum? No? that's okay, we'll try to get some distress flares for him to take. Should do the trick.

My sons hunt in packs, banter and insults bouncing off each other that would be the envy of any Mock The Week panel. Sensing a slightly wounded animal (aka The Mothership) they went in for the kill.

Let's all make a bet as to which part of the motorway he phones us up and says She's Driving Me Mad & I've Left Her In A Layby !

James actually gets my road map of Great Britain out and they all start circling towns, one of them only 3 miles from Mr O's home.

I started to clear away the buffet feeling very much Pissed Off & Offended. This lot did not deserve any more spring rolls or wagon wheels.

A few days later another bestie Jan popped in and I made

light of the scathing comments from the offspring . She is the most practical woman on God's planet.

Well, Fairy. Get him to kick you out at Warwick Services. The toilets there are beautiful.

Ummm thanks for the tip. But do they sell Haggis?????

Author's note: *We didn't get to Scotland on that occasion as the holiday was cancelled due to the funds needed to replace the car. We had our first and only holiday five years later when we were gifted a 2 night stay by his daughter Georgia. It was in Scotland and it's still a magical memory for me.*

PS: Still laughing every time I write author.

MAY

Nul Points

Portugal is beautiful. The weather glorious, the people genuinely friendly and the exquisite tiles and ironwork everywhere fascinating.

And the food !! Heaven on a plate every time. The sea food is amazing. I'm as happy as Dory, so to speak. I ate some sea bass so perfect that I told the 78 year old chef I'd marry him. I wasn't joking either.

Dear Sweet Lord the puddings.....I've invented Breakfast Puddings. They're officially a thing now.

However, a point of interest I've noticed.

Slices of life

The Portuguese at the hotel enjoy music with accompained accordian to a female vocalist who went into an enthusiastic rendition of God Knows What.

All sixteen songs sounded the same and had the identical pulsating beat the accordian. To be fair, the Portuguese guests were going crazy with love for both singer and songs and they all danced marvellously well. It was like watching Strictly. No dancing around your handbags here.

Then the clapping started. More claps than a clinic. Endless night.

Mamma bloody Mia, they clapped along as they danced.

Jan and I sat there transfixed.

Oh and Endless Joy. Today at the poolside, the same singer did an encore of the whole album. By the third song in, Jan and I were plotting her demise.....which would involve the swimming pool, lead weights and the microphone.

When I spoke to Mr O on the phone before dinner, he asked if there was a toddler having a tantrum near our balcony that he could hear?

Nope, that noise was Portugal's answer to Adele, bless her heart.

Explains why we never win at Eurovision anymore though. Not enough accordians.

JUNE

Beach Babes & Water-melons

Today we decided to swim in the sea because a: it's just across the road from our hotel and b: we needed the sea water to work it's magic due to both being badly bitten by the entire mosquito population of Rhodes.

Insanely itchy !! In Braille my legs would resemble a copy of The Reader's Digest.

Beach extremely pebbley (is that a word? Pebbley? Anyway it was like Chesil Beach but with nearby Moussaka)

Even with sandals on, feet and pebbles and the tide were

all fighting against each other to claim our downfall.

Actually that combination plus gravity succeeded in the end. Both of us went arse over tit into the sea.

We shrieked with laughter and tried to find a shred of dignity which had probably floated out to sea, nearly followed by our sandals before we rescued them.

Getting out of the water was just as unsteady, Jan ahead of me until she came a cropper and bum in the air, fell again. All I'll say is that I definitely saw next week's washing.

When we got back onto our towels we were still laughing like braying donkeys, absolutely all dignity lost. And not for the first time, I might add.

After lunch, we had a swim in the hotel pool (water still ice cold, time to negotiate with David Attenborough for Frozen Planet 3) and some idiot guy stands on the side of the infinity pool. Behind him is Nothing. No bean bags to bounce off or soft pillows to break his fall. just concrete ten foot down.

As Jan observed, If he falls he'll have a head caved in like a watermelon.

When he spoke to the manager (who told him to get down you'll break your bloody neck you tool or words to that effect) we realised he was a Brit. And an arrogant one too.

The rest of us watched with much delight mixed with morbid fascination at the drama unfolding. It was as riveting as the Den & Angie Divorce Christmas Special.

The prat was told No More Alcohol ! Much in the same tone as Shortround telling Indiana Jones: No More Parachutes !!!

He got very rude and sweary to the bar staff, pool staff and the poor lass on reception. All the other Brits kept apologising on behalf of King and Country.

Management told him very firmly that any further bad behaviour he would be confined to his room. Rest of us looked smug.

At dinner he tried to order booze with his meal and royally kicked off again at the refusal.

Jan and I took AGES eating our meal because it was fascinating entertainment. She said Go and get a bit more pudding so we can watch some more.

I came back with cherry cheesecake.

The other choice had been watermelon.

JULY

And A Starter For 10

Today we went on on a day trip to Myra, saw a sea turtle and met Mehmet Tus.

Tus was a genius. He was our guide and he knew EVERYTHING, EVER.

I had astounded Jan earlier in the week by knowing all of The Waltons from John Boy down to Elizabeth in order of ages. I bet Tus could have us all the names of the production crew too.

On the coach, he told us about every species of trees from Antalya to Myra. This guy should have his own television show.

While waiting for the other passengers (who were rudely an hour late) we got some fresh air and he cheerfully informed us that Turkey still had wolves and bears.

Oh really? How very interesting (taking a few discreet steps nearer to the safety of thr coach)

Our stop for breakfast (we'd been collected from the hotel at half six) was at a little village and Tus obviously knew the family who were our hosts. Was he the Turkish equivalent of a Godfather to the second eldest boy? I expect so.

The boat trip was sensational. No other word for it.

Another group were already aboard when we arrived and their guide was very excitable. He was a Frenchman who yelled his explanations and to be honest (and not very PC) reminded me of old film footage of The Nuremberg Rally.

Which is why Tus told us very quietly to his group of 11

that he'd just spotted a sea turtle gently swimming near the boat. We all watched this beautiful creature in awe. I'd never seen one in the wild before and I was enchanted.

Our boat trip continued to show us a sunken city on the island of Kekova and Tus gave us a full run down on the history of everything we saw, not once referring to notes. Every building on every island, bits of rock that looked like bits of rock but were in fact ancient stones with fascinating history, Tus knew them all.

When we stopped for a swim, Tus pointed out each rock known to be inhabited by sea urchins. I honestly would not have batted an eyelid if he'd announced he was best pals with The Little Mermaid.

After lunch, we went to Myra and The Church of St Nicholas. Tranquil, beautiful and spiritual. Tus told us about each room, the history of Christianity in Turkey and why this place is so special to Russian tourists. It was incredible to see so much of it still standing after centuries.

Truly humbling.

Our last stop were the Rock Tombs and amphitheatre. Not often I'm lost for words, as you know, but I'd never seen anything like it.

The French shouty guide was giving his group a lecture. Hope they were taking notes as I expect he was going to test them afterwards (less than an 80% pass and they have to walk home)

Tus, of course gave us a quieter and I suspect, more informative talk about tombs and the amphitheatre. Our group were in awe.

We could hear the French bloke yelling Sacrifice ! Sarcifice !

I thought Shit, someone's failed their exam, poor sod.

Tus explained that centuries ago goverments officials might be sacrificed if not doing their job well.

Blimey, that'll be most of ours these days then. The list would make The Doomsday Book look like a raffle ticket.

Our brilliant guide also described his childhood and life in rural Turkey. He didn't mention that he'd read The Boys' Book of Knowledge from the age of 2 but I betcha he had. Plus Encyclopaedia Britannica for every birthday.

What a memorable day, all of the sights and sounds of the history and seeing my first sea turtle.

And finding my new best buddy for every pub quiz EVER.

AUGUST

Turkey, It's Not Just For Christmas

Well well well, it's been a (Robin)Day of Questions (Time) today.

 Oh excellent pun there, Mary.

First was Jan's at breakfast this mornig as we surveyed the display of fruit:

Blimey, you ever seen plums That Big before?!

I had not.

In the sea, it was time for Aqua Zumba again. The instructor took off his shirt and 30 menopausal women stood and gawped and prayed to Neptune that their tits would stay in their swimsuits with all the bobbing about.

Zumba Hunk yells at me to keep up with the moves. Believe me it was enough hard work to keep bloody upright in the sea, let alone do co-ordinated stuff.

Lift your legs in time to zee beat! he shouts.

I thought Fuck off I haven't SEEN my legs for years. (I think Fernando by Abba were No.1)

Then we were told to tie our woggle in a knot. Jan couldn't tie hers properly and he bloody gave her His woggle.

At this moment I began to question our friendship, quite frankly. She was waving His woggle around that he'd had a hold of a few minutes ago.

I mean where's the loyalty?

That woggle could have been my souvenier on the whole trip instead of fridge magnets.

My doubts about her continued into the afternoon when I went shopping to bring back something for the lads. They're not fashion label snobs and we found a t-shirt shop full of genuine fakes. Ideal.

The owner told me he would knock 100 lire off if Jan gave him a kiss.

I did some mental maths and worked out what she'd have to do to him for me to get 6 t-shirts and 3 hoodies basically free but she flatly refused his advances.

Friends ?! I ask you !!

The last question today was How Much Do I Value My Life?

We had a lift in a Vehicle of Death. It was basically half a mobility scooter but with a motorbike attached to the front.

During the three minute journey I recited: The Lord Is My Shepherd

Slices of life

Hail Mary (twice)

Shine Jesus Shine.

The driver was called Carlos and he played the jolly game of Let's Race The Public Transport. I'm not saying we were close to the bus but I swear I could see the driver's nose hair.

I honestly thought Okay, so this is how I'm going to die. Damn and I've just settled into my flat too.

When we finally reached our destination I got off and kissed the ground like the Pope does when he arrives in a new country.

I nearly died without holding anyone's woggle for quite a few years.

Tragic.

SEPTEMBER

The Chronicles of Chania

What a glorious day. We'd booked to go on a boat trip and not a cloud in the sky to be seen. Weather warning on my phone said It's Gonna Be Friggin Hot.

Boat not called Titanic or Poseidon so all good there too.

Our captain was Yannis. His Mr Smee/crew was his nephew Nicolai. They greeted us with huge smiles of welcome, bless their hearts.

26 passengers in total, mostly English but some Italian too and a couple from Sweden.

Before we've even left the port, ol' Bjorn's missus was sorting herself a pair of flippers from the boat's supply. Never mind about about anyone else, she wasn't missing out. Bet she never queues in Ikea either.

Yannis was full of information including the astonishing (to me anyrate) that the mountains in Crete get snow capped in winter. Don't you just love learning something new and unexpected?

We stopped in the first bay for a swim. I had to take a woggle in with me just for reassurance in the deep water. It was wonderfully warm and so clear.

Flippin' Freda the Flipper Thief jumped in, obviously all geared up. I didn't care. I was trying to do calm breathing and clutch me woggle like it was the last Curly Wurly on God's Earth. My phobia of deep water is immense.

Back on board, Yannis asked me if I was Greek because he said I looked very Greek (albeit a pale one)

I was over the moon. I mean I'm very proud of my Irish roots but have felt for some time that my spiritual home is The Land Of Moussaka.

Some daft cow (woman not farm animal) had gone too near the rocks during her swim and had cut her finger. Serves her right. Don't play on the rocks, it's a written rule.

I said: Oh just hold your hand up and apply some pressure, it'll soon stop bleeding.

But nah, she suddenly sees herself as a Shirley Valentine and a budding romance with Yannis is on the cards. She starts whimpering: Ooh Yannis do you have a plaster? Ooh Yannis you're ever so gentle !

Poor Yannis was mentionig his wife & kids at every opportunity, but ol' Shirl was a determined gal.

Mary and Jan a little less sympathic: Just swim again soon and the sea water is the best antiseptic ever.

Slices of life

Nicolai swam off and brought back some live sea urchins for us to hold. It's like holding a heavy spider (but with a billion more legs) So fascinating. We were thrilled.

Shiley declined to hold it, obviously due to her injuries. Judi Dench, eat your heart out and give that woman an Oscar.

Another swim stop and I braved it without the woggle. Unbelievably proud of myself.

Jan goes into the water without making a splash, elegant as you like. Shirley declined another swim.

Good point, we told her, Sharks can smell blood......

Now that I know that I'm very obviously Greek, I had another raki after my final swim. Couldn't move my feet for 30 minutes afterwards but otherwise all good.

On the way back to Kalyves, Miss Valentine's leaning over Yannis, with her boobs nearly resting on his shoulder as he was sitting down. She'd asked to see his map (yeah like she's suddenly bloody Lord Nelson! FFS) and it was clear that she was hoping to get the Come Hither from him.

Take it from me, Shirl. He ain't interested. That polite but very slight embarrassment aura he's giving off? Love, I've had decades of that from guys. It's not gonna happen for ya. Nadda.

As we were disembarking, the only Getting Off she was gonna get today ha ha, she giggled and said coyly:

Oh Yannis it must be wonderful to have a job where everyone loves you !

Jan and I had that conversation two women can have without saying a word - Fucking hell, woman he doesn't fancy you and you've lost all dignity now piss off !

What a beautiful day. I will always remember it. A snapshot in my mind to keep. Shit. Just had a thought. Do you think Yannis thought I was Greek because of my moustache?

OCTOBER

A Symphony of Autumn

I'll start with a confession. I adore Autumn. It's my favourite time of year with the crispness of a clear day, the velvet darkness of early mornings, the need for more hot chocolate instead of a mere cup of tea.

Every year I fall in love in love with the thought of my winter wardrobe, picturing myself as a stylish Nigella or heading for Balmoral in casual but oh so stylish tartan and tweeds. In truth I always end up looking like Big Lady Meets Yeti.

Sorry, I digress.

The highlight of Autumn for me, which even surpasses cinnamon buns, are the extraordinary colours that scatter throughout our gardens and countryside. The palettes of yellows, burnished copper, rustic reds and every shade inbetween are a joy to behold and no more so than on Brownsea Island.

The place is beautiful throughout the year, of course. Spring heralds the carpets of daffodils fields (such a gloriously happy flower, don't you think?) and because of Brownsea's beds of dancing yellow these will always be my favourite flower, bar none.

The clear blue summer skies and lush green pastures provide the perfect setting for picnics and family memories can be made and treasured. My love of Shakespeare came from watching The Open Air Theatre each year, the Church Field echoing with poetic sonnets and a billion mosquitoes.

But Autumn on Brownsea is magical. Mother Nature has her finest palette at hand and it is a feast for the eyes and truly medicine for the soul.

Majestic horse chestnut trees (climbed as a child till my fear of heights got the better of me) display a wondrous floor of great sways of golden leaves and those ultimate weapons of old, conkers.

The mighty oaks lord it along the pathways, scattering their acorns underfoot adding to the crunching sounds of the Autumnal Symphony.

I defy anyone not to want to kick through those russet leaves. The sounds will transport you back to a flood of memories. Also I definitely recommend wearing wellinton boots. They simply yell Adventure, don't you think? And this season can be so unpredictable weather wise that wellies give you that added protection in Very Deep Mud. Always a bonus.

The viewpoints above the South Shore enable breathless

sights across Poole Harbour and the rolling hills of the Purbecks. The gorse and heather along Brownsea's cliff tops are sublime against crisp, clear days where you do indeed feel like you can see forever.

In all the places I've ever visited, Autumn is summed up in the quiet but spectacular fashion of The Lily Pond. It is tucked away between the daffodil fields and Middle Street. It's path is a serenade of copper leaves and the Lily Pond itself appears surrounded by pillars of trees and a serenity rarely found in today's bustling world. The water's reflections highlights the stillness around it. A sanctuary to me growing up among the masterpiece of nature. No sounds to be heard except for the birdsong of the island's inhabitants and the rustling of autumnal breezes throught the leaves and occasionally the scampering of the red squirrels collecting their stores.

I used to sit here. And just be.

As I said, it was medicine for the soul.

I am not a very travelled person, compared to some. But I cannot imagine a more perfect setting in which to breath in the season.

Even beats hot chocolate and cinnamon buns.

Authors note: *Not wishing to put a downer on this rather poetic piece I've written, but The Lily Pond from always being my favourite place very nearly became my last place too. I suddenly had major changes to deal with, coupled with heartbreak and a complete lack of self confidence and my mental health (already very fragile) went into a dark place.*

My plan was to go to the Lily Pond and just sit there until I expired. One of my besties Aurora sussed something was up and phoned me every 15 minutes. In the end, I didn't even get on the boat to the island, thankfully.

For those who need it: Samaritans - 116 123

NOVEMBER

Author's note: *This is based on a neighbour of my Grandparents. Even as a child, I was fascinated by her as she didn't draw breath during her visits and wore the same mac, come rain or shine. Now I've realised that the poor lady was a hoarder but in those days everyone in the cul de sac very much down on her. I've written it as she spoke so take a deep breath !*

The two pairs of knickers gem was not from the same woman but a genuine means of deterrent used by another lady not wishing to get pregnant again & she's still using it 45 years on to ensure he keeps to his side of the bed. Too amazing not to include it.

Two Pairs of Knickers

Morning Vi, I'm not stopping- just popped in to see if you've heard ol' Mother Bridges got taken ill last night andher son-what's he called? Arthur? Albert? Alan? Anyway, him had to call an ambulance at gone midnight and she's been taken up to the General and she hasn't come back yet. No I'm not stopping Vi. You okay, Frank? Garden looking lovely even this time of year. Mine's only got marigolds in it , even I can't kill them. Not in your way,Vi? Wash day, eh? that's a good ol' boiler you've got there. That's what Reg used to call me, his old boiler. No I'm not stopping. Oh you off to the greenhouse, Frank? No I'm not stopping. Oh a cup of tea be lovely thanks Vi so long I'm not in the way. No I don't really have a wash day I just wash out me smalls in the kitchen sink as it's only me now- don't bother too much. Yeah me mac could do with a bit of Fairy Snow, you're right. Lovely cup of tea, Vi thanks ever so. No I'm not stopping. I bought this mac inBobby's in '56 I think. Our Renee was still in her pram. Yeah I think you're right Vi, don't think it's ever been washed. Well it's only me, isn't it? Renee never pops in now, says the papers upsets her. Doesn't upset me it's comfy isn't it, having newspapers about the place, more homely like. Mind you Vi yours is like a palace. How's your Christine? Still Ward Sister up at the hospital? She might hear about Mrs Bridges and if it's fatal. And your Barry? Still doing the boat thing? I see they always call in to see you on thursdays-that's nice for you Vi. No I'm not stopping. Oh another cup of tea would be lovely ta very much. I think you're very brave having two kiddies-after our Renee was born I said to Reg No More Shenanigans I'm not going through that again. So I tell you what I did Vi, I put two pairs of knickers on every night, one thin pair and one really thick. He tried of course but I had my armour on and he couldn't get past it. How long for, Vi ? Oh about 20 years till he passed on. Two pairs of knickers that's the answer Vi. Lunch smells nice Vi, no I don't bother much meself, well there's only me now and there's still some streaky rashers in the pan from yesterday so that'll do. Got it from Shergold's last week and some eggs somewhere but can't quite find them, probably under me Daily Express. Or baked beans, got loads of them Vi. Good to stock up isn't it. And pilchards. Your cat is always at the back door when I'm having pilchards I can hear him meowing, don't know how he knows cos I never open a window and with the papers he can't see in at the windows but he always knows. Lovely cat, such company. Frank's a long time in the greenhouse, Vi. No I'm not stopping. Going off now to see Mrs Holt at number 4 and to Shergolds for some pilchards and..... me Daily Express.

DECEMBER

If.......Three Wise Women?

Geraldine was distinctly uncomfortable. The camel was purposely rocking, she was sure. She was hot and sweaty and had a severe case of PMT. Despite being several feet off the ground, the sand in Got Everywhere.

"Are you sure we're going the right way?" she asked irritably.

"Yes. We. Are. Do you want some cheese with your constant whine?" frowned Anthea getting, frankly fed up with Geraldine's complaining.

Slices of life

Geraldine made a face at Anthea's back and promised herself to feed Anthea's camel some very dodgy grapes for the journey home.

Maud reached down into her bag and pulled out her thermos.

"Anyone fancy a cuppa? I've got a mouth here drier than Herod's flipflops."

They stopped for a brew and enjoyed a couple of chocolate hobnobs.

Maud looked up at the sky, "That star's still going nicely. Reckon we'll be there in about half an hour."

"What's Bethlehem like?" asked Anthea. "I've never been. Bert always pumps for a city break to Jerusalem."

"Not bad," observed Maud, "But not one decent wool shop. Shocking when you think how many shepherds we've passed. Exports!!!"

They all agreed. All faces in complete unison of total

disapproval.

Much as Maud predicted, they soon reached the suburbs of Bethlehem. The sight of them caused quite a stir. Children stared as they rode past and many innkeepers wished they'd had spare rooms to offer. These ladies looked like they weren't short of a few bob or two.

Maud halted her camel abruptly next to one of the innkeepers, the star shining directly over his establishment. Her voice was one of Commander In Chief.

"We're looking for a newborn baby. Parents are from Nazareth. Look sharp. We haven't got all day."

Under Maud's formidable stare, the poor man was temporily struck dumb. He eventually managed to stammer "Yeah...yes they're in in mmmy stable around the back...I had no room... I... "

His explanation trailed off as three pairs of eyes glared at him like flint.

Slices of life

They verbally tore him to shreds.

"In the stable?! In the bloody stable?! And what are you sleeping on, we may well ask? Oh don't bother with your reply now, it's a bed no doubt. You couldn't get off your arse and give an expectant mother a proper bed?"

Geraldine leant over to the shaking man and whispered menacingly to him "Wait till we put your inn on Tripadvisor later. Our review will make it famous but Not In A Good Way. Now where's this stable?"

He pointed to behind his (soon to be crumbling) business. The women swiftly dismounted and parked their camels. They collected their bags and made their way to the stable.

Three bustling in as One, they scanned the scene rather like a barcode. A young woman was laying on a makeshift bed of hay, looking tired but serenely happy. Her small newborn son lay sleeping in her arms. Her husband sat next to her, gazing adoringly at them both.

"Well just don't sit there, young man! Mother needs a cup of tea. Put the kettle on!"

Joseph jumped out of his skin at the barked orders. Had he suddenly acquired three bossy in laws?

He mumbled something about wasn't it supposed to be Three Wise Men?

Maud snorted. "Man flu" she stated shortly. "Now get that fire lit."

Joseph wanted to point out that surely even a small fire in a stable full of straw was maybe not the best idea? But he didn't dare. Even Herod would be terrified of Maud, he was sure.

Geraldine and Anthea unpacked their bags, full of gifts. Their first were Marigold gloves along with cilit bang. They set to scrubbing that stable until even the oxen shone.

They gave Mary some myrrh lotion for her stretchmarks ,

ideal for nappy rash too.

All three ladies cooed over the baby, now sleeping in a clean manger, wrapped in blankets handed down from Anthea's daughter's boy, Matthew.

Geraldine gently stroking the wisps of baby's hair asked:

"What are you going to call him?"

"Jesus," said Mary, softly.

The older women exchanged glances.

"Er.....right. Well now...that's different. Have you thought of Thomas ? Or Samuel, maybe? I hear the name Hugh Jackman is very popular these days."

"His name is Jesus" said Mary a little more firmly. Maud rolled her eyes. That's the trouble with these young gals, they hear an unusual name and go with it. I mean whoever is going to remember the name Jesus it'll never catch on. Poor little mite.

The fire was going nicely now and Anthea unpacked a casserole pot and told Joseph to heat it up

"It's my own personal recipe" she said proudly.

"Not unless you've changed your name to Delia Smith, it isn't," muttered Maud.

Geraldine gave Mary some frankincense air freshener.

"It's stronger than Febreze and you'll need it with all these animals. We haven't got any animals in the house at home but our Keith after a bowl of couscous could put a camel into a coma."

They also unpacked nappies and vests and woolly vests plus soap and shampoo and chocolate for Mary.

Despite Joseph looking hopeful of some manly treats for him, all he was presented with was a detailed timetable for the care of wife and child and a bag of barley sugars. He didn't dare complain. Wise man.

The ladies collected their now empty bags, preparing to

leave. They were met at the stable entrance by shepherds coming to visit the new family. Maud beamed at them.

"Welcome, welcome. Wipe your feet!"

As they trundled back to their camels, Anthea looked at her companions.

"Shall I say what I KNOW we're ALL thinking?"

The other two nodded.

"That baby looks nothing like his father."

Mary-Frances Hewlett

Slices of life

Printed in Great Britain
by Amazon